WESTMINSTER SCHOOLS

PRESENTED BY

Tom POWELL

1986

SMYTHE GAMBRELL
LIBRARY

Kelly S.

A New True Book

POND LIFE

By Lynn M. Stone

This "true book" was prepared
under the direction of
Illa Podendorf,
formerly with the Laboratory School.
University of Chicago

CHILDRENS PRESS, CHICAGO

Pond with snow white lilies

PHOTO CREDITS

Lynn Stone—Cover, 2, 7, 11, 12 (2 photos), 14, 17, 19 (4 photos), 20 (2 photos), 21, 23 (3 photos), 24 (2 photos), 26 (2 photos), 27, 28, 29, 30, 31 (2 photos, top), 33, 36, 38 (left), 40 (3 photos), 41

Jerry Hennen—4, 8, 9, 10, 15, 16 (2 photos), 31 (bottom left), 34, 37, 38 (right), 39 (2 photos), 43

James P. Rowan—44

Cover: Canada geese on a pond

Library of Congress Cataloging in Publication Data

Stone, Lynn M.
  Pond life.

  (A New true book)
  Includes index.
  Summary: Briefly describes how ponds are formed and examines the plant and animal life these small bodies of still water support.
  1. Pond ecology—Juvenile literature. [1. Pond ecology. 2. Ecology] I. Title.
QH541.5.P63S76 1983   574.5'26322   83-7311
ISBN 0-516-01705-5   AACR2

TABLE OF CONTENTS

The Pond. . . 5

Ponds Are Important. . . 9

Plants and Animals of the
    Pond. . . 12

The Pond Shore. . . 15

The Deeper Pond. . . 24

Winter. . . 35

Spring. . . 36

Summer. . . 39

Autumn. . . 41

Remember the Pond. . . 43

Words You Should Know. . . 46

Index. . . 47

Beaver pond, Jackson Hole, Wyoming

THE POND

Ponds are bodies of still water. Lakes are like ponds. But lakes are larger, deeper, and older.

Each pond is different. Some are much larger than others. Some are colder or deeper than others.

Ponds are found in many places. Some old ponds are "natural." They were made thousands of years ago by giant mountains of ice called glaciers. Other natural ponds were left when rivers changed their paths.

Backyard pond

Many ponds are new. They were made by people.

One way to make a pond is to block the flow of a stream or river. The water backs up, making a pond.

The wall that blocks a stream is called a dam. Some pond water pours over the dam.

Beavers make ponds, too. They cut down trees with their sharp teeth. Then they put tree limbs across streams. Water backs up and a pond is made.

Beaver dam

PONDS ARE IMPORTANT

We have many uses for ponds. Clean ponds are good places to swim or fish. They are also places to row boats and paddle canoes.

Farmers often make ponds for their animals. Farm animals need water to drink.

Some farmers raise fish. Most fish farmers raise catfish or trout. These are fish that people like to catch and eat.

Mill pond

People used to dam streams and make mill ponds.

A long time ago, ponds were used for ice. People bought ice to keep their food fresh.

PLANTS AND ANIMALS OF THE POND

Many wild animals use ponds, too. Some of these animals hunt for food at the pond. Sometimes they just come for a drink.

White tail deer (right) and bison (below) drink at ponds.

Remember: each pond is different. The plants and animals in each pond are also different.

All ponds, though, have many tiny plants and animals. Many of them are so small they can be seen only under a microscope.

These tiny plants and animals are important. They are food for other animals.

All animals need food

Fishing spider on duckweed, a floating pond plant.

to live. Many of the bigger pond animals eat the smaller animals.

Not all pond animals eat other animals, however. Some eat only plants. A few animals will eat animals or plants!

THE POND SHORE

The water at the edge of the pond is not deep. Many plants grow here.

This area, where water and land meet, is called the shore.

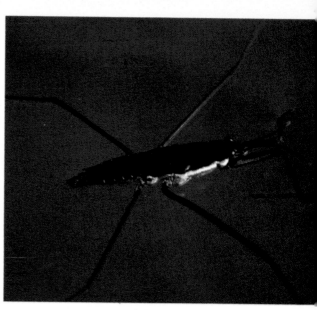

The damselfly (above) and water strider (right) are pond insects.

Some plants float. Their roots do not reach the bottom. The duckweed is a tiny floating plant. Ducks eat duckweed.

Many insects live in the pond. They are food for little fish, frogs, toads, and salamanders.

16

Frogs, toads, and salamanders are born in the pond. They grow up there. But they leave the water when they are adults.

Frogs stay close to the pond.

Bullfrog. All frogs have webbed toes and long, strong back legs. They are good swimmers and jumpers.

Toads and salamanders come back to the pond each spring. They lay their eggs in the water.

Then the toads hop into fields and woods. The salamanders stay in wet places near the pond.

Frogs, salamanders, toads, fish, and bugs are food for snakes.

The garter snake hunts

Top left: American toad
Top right: Common water snake
Bottom left: Garter snake
Bottom right: Tiger salamander

along the shore of the
pond. The water snake
hunts in the pond.

Above: Great blue heron
Right: Green heron on water lettuce plant

Long-legged birds walk in the shallow water near shore. They are called wading birds.

Wading birds use their long, sharp bills to spear food. They eat fish, frogs, and even snakes.

Raccoon hunting at daybreak

The pond's marshy edge
is a busy place.
Raccoons come to hunt
animals in the mud.
Small birds called
sandpipers hunt mud
animals, too.

21

Some kinds of ducks
eat plants and catch little
animals near the pond
shore. These ducks can
tip upside down to feed!
Wild geese and swans
can also tip upside down.
This is called "bobbing"
for food.

Wild geese and swans
have long necks. They
can bob in deeper water.

The pond plants are
good hiding places.

Top left: Crayfish are related to
              lobsters.
Top right: Canada goose in its
              nest
Left: Mute swan bobs for food

Clams live among the roots.
Snails live on the stems.
Beetles, worms, and
crayfish live here, too.
   Many kinds of birds
nest in the shore plants.

THE DEEPER POND

Away from the marshy shore the water is deeper. Pond lily plants grow here. Their stems are like long straws. They may be longer than you are tall. The stems

Red water lily

Yellow water lily

connect the flower to
the roots. The roots are
in the mud.

Many large fish live here.
The fish eat plants and
animals. Often they catch
insects that land on the
water.

If small fish come to
the deep pond, they may
be eaten by the larger fish.

Fish are good
swimmers. But there are
other good swimmers in
the pond. One of the
best is the otter.

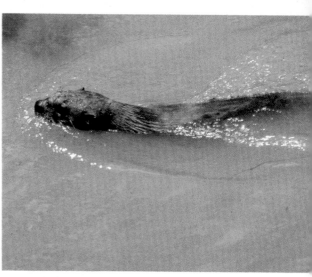

Otters have thick, brown fur. They are the size of a large cat. They have sleek bodies and tails.

Otters are land animals, but they can hold their breath for a long time underwater.

Otters swim faster than most fish. When they come to the pond, otters catch fish.

Painted turtle

Turtles are good swimmers, too. They cannot catch fast fish, but they eat sick and dead fish. Turtles will eat almost anything. They help keep the pond clean.

Common snapping turtle. Inside its jaws is a pink tongue. Fish think the tongue is a worm. When fish come near, the snapping turtle grabs them with its powerful jaws

Turtles like deep water. Turtles leave the pond only to sun themselves or lay eggs.

One of the largest pond animals is the snapping turtle.

In ponds in the southern United States you might find another

When an alligator is not hungry, it may even share its log with a turtle!

animal with strong jaws:
the alligator.

Alligators eat turtles.
Sometimes they catch
big fish or birds.

Alligators sun
themselves like turtles
do.

A water turkey spreads its wings to dry.

A few birds hunt in deep water. One of these is the water turkey or snakebird.

The water turkey has a long neck and a sharp bill. It has webbed feet to help it swim.

The water turkey dives underwater. It spears fish with its beak.

Top left: Mallard duck
Left: Coot defends its
nest
Above: Pied-billed grebe

Grebes and coots are diving birds, too. Grebes have short, sharp beaks. They look very much like ducks. Grebs catch little fish. Coots eat plant and animal food.

31

Some kinds of ducks can dive. They do not bob for food like their cousins. These ducks can catch plants and animals in deep water.

The fish hawk has very sharp eyes. It can see fish in the pond far below.

When the fish hawk sees a large fish, it folds its wings and dives.

Fish hawk
or osprey

The fish hawk has claws, called talons, on its toes. The claws grab the fish and the hawk flies away.

Frozen beaver pond

WINTER

Each winter ice covers the pond. The pond is quiet. Insects and small animals are hidden in the mud below water and ice.

The ice protects many of these animals. The water under the ice is cold. But it is not as cold as the winter air.

The dragonfly eats other insects.

SPRING

In spring animals that spent the winter in the mud crawl out. Larger plants begin to grow. More and more insects appear.

Shrimp and other tiny creatures with shells appear, too.

Newly hatched coot in its nest

Birds fly to the pond. Some build nests. Some rest for a few days. Then they fly farther north.

Each spring many baby animals are born at the pond.

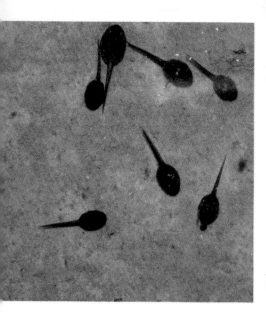
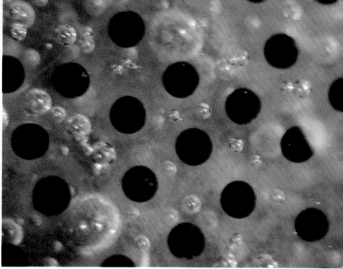

Above: Eggs of green frog
Left: Tadpoles

Baby birds hatch from eggs in nests. Baby frogs and toads, called tadpoles, hatch from eggs in the water.

Baby fish are called fry. They hatch from eggs, too. They are born in shallow water.

SUMMER

The babies of spring
grow up in the summer.
Young birds learn to fly
and find their own food.
Young raccoons and
otters learn to hunt.

Left: Raccoon hunting in a pond
Below: Young yellow-headed blackbird

Cattails grow tall and green. Flowers of pond lilies and other green plants bloom.

Above: White water lily
Right: Pickerelweed and butterfly
Below: Cattail

Canada geese migrating

AUTUMN

In autumn the pond
water becomes cooler as
air above the pond cools.
Plants begin to die. There
are fewer of the tiny,
unseen plants and animals
in the pond.

41

Soon the pond will freeze. Soon it will be winter again.

Pond animals prepare for winter. Most birds fly south. The muskrat and the beaver store plants in their dens. Frogs burrow into the mud at the bottom of the pond. Turtles and many smaller animals dig into the mud.

Blacktail Pond, Grand Teton Park

REMEMBER THE POND

The pond is a fairly
small body of still water.
The pond is like a
busy city. But instead of
people, many plants and
animals live at the pond.

43

Nine-mile Pond, Everglades National Park

44

Each one helps the pond to be healthy. Each one is important. Even the tiny plants and animals that you can't see are important.

A healthy pond is an exciting place to visit.

WORDS YOU SHOULD KNOW

burrow(BER • oh) — to dig a hole or tunnel into the ground

coot(KOOT) — a diving bird

dam — a wall built across a river or other body of water

den — the home for a wild animal

duckweed(DUK • weed) — a plant with small green leaves that grows on water

fry — baby fish

glacier(GLAY • sher) — a large mass of moving ice and snow

grebe(GREEB) — a diving bird

marsh — an area of low, wet land

mill pond — a body of water that is used to make a wheel, attached to a mill, turn

otter(OT • er) — a mammal with webbed feet and thick brown fur that lives in or near water

salamander(SAL • ah • man • der) — an amphibian

shallow(SHAL • oh) — not deep

sleek — smooth and shiny

still(STIHL) — quiet; not moving

talon(TAL • un) — the claw of an animal

wade(WAYDE) — to walk in water

webbed — having skin or thin tissue that connects the toes

INDEX

alligators, 29
animals, 8, 10, 12-14, 16-23, 25-29, 35-39, 42, 43, 45
autumn, 41, 42
baby animals, 37
baby birds, 38
baby fish, 38
baby frogs, 38
baby toads, 38
beavers, 8, 42
beetles, 23
birds, 20-23, 29-33, 37-39, 42
boating, 9
bobbing for food, 22
bugs, 18
catfish, 10
cattails, 40
clams, 23
claws, 33
coots, 31
crayfish, 23
dams, 8, 11
deep ponds, 24-33
diving birds, 30-33
ducks, 16, 22, 32,
duckweed, 16

farming, 10
fish, 10, 16, 18, 20, 25-27, 29-33, 38
fish farming, 10
fish hawks, 32, 33
fishing, 9
floating plants, 16
frogs, 16-18, 20, 38, 42
fry, 38
garter snakes, 18
geese, 22
glaciers, 6
grebes, 31
hawks, 32, 33
ice, 11, 35
insects, 16, 35, 36
lakes, 5
lily plants, 24, 40
long-legged birds, 20
making ponds, 5-8
microscopes, 13
mill ponds, 11
muskrats, 42
natural ponds, 6
new ponds, 7, 8
old ponds, 6

otters, 25, 26, 39
plants, 13-16, 22-25, 36, 40-43, 45
raccoons, 21, 39
rivers, 6, 7
salamanders, 16-18
sandpipers, 21
shore, 15-23
shrimp, 36
snails, 23
snakebirds, 30
snakes, 18-20
snapping turtles, 28
spring, 18, 36-38
streams, 7, 8, 11

summer, 39, 40
swans, 22
swimming, 9
tadpoles, 38
talons, 33
toads, 16-18, 38
trout, 10
turtles, 27-29, 42
uses for ponds, 9-11
wading birds, 20
water snakes, 19
water turkeys, 30
winter, 35, 42
worms, 23

About the Author

Lynn M. Stone was born and raised in Meriden, Connecticut. He received his undergraduate degree from Aurora College in Illinois and his master's degree from Northern Illinois University. Once a teacher in Sarasota, Florida, Mr. Stone currently teaches English to junior high school students in the West Aurora Public School system.

A free-lance wildlife photographer and journalist, Lynn has had his work appear in many publications including National Wildlife, Ranger Rick, Oceans, Country Gentleman, Animal Kingdom, *and* International Wildlife. *He has also contributed to Time-Life, National Geographic, Audubon Field Guide, and Hallmark Cards publications.*

Many of Lynn Stone's photographs have been used in the New True Books published by Childrens Press.